R U N C O R N

A Town Not So New

by
H.F. Starkey

To Norma

Published by:
MiddleView

miview**dle**

an imprint of Avid Publications.
Middleview
New Road, GWESPYR
Flintshire
CH8 9LS
Tel (44) : 01745   886769
e-mail: info@Middleview.co.uk.
www. AvidPublications.co.uk

Edited by William David Roberts MA
Typsetting © Middleview / Avid Publications
Cover design by Janice Rickards

Other books and DVDs from MiddleView and AVID are detailed
at the rear of this book.
These can be obtained direct from AVID / MIDDLEVIEW on:
Tel : (44) 01745 886769

or e-mail to : info@Middleview.co.uk
www. Avidpublications.co.uk

RUNCORN

A Town Not So New

ACKNOWLEDGEMENTS

For photographs and information I wish to acknowledge the help
afforded to me by :-

George Aspinwall
Steven Ball
Margaret Bold
Bernard Buckle
Ross Bullock
Les Carlisle
James Collins
Alex Cowan
Percy Dunbavand
Kathleen Edwards
Roy Gamon
Roy Gough
Catherine Hall
Evelyn Hayes
John Hodgson
Fred Horsefield
Peter Johnson

Christopher Kelly
Bill Leathwood
Philip Littlemore
Brenda McCormack
Ray Miller
John Rathbone
Alan Roberts
Ada Rooney
Geoff Perry
Ernest Silcock
James Starkey
John Thompson
Aubrey Teare
Peter Vardy
Ann Walker
Teresa Walker
David Williams

INTRODUCTION

In 1964, under the New Towns Act, a designation order was made to create a new town at Runcorn which would provide housing and employment for people from Liverpool and north Merseyside. The population in 1964 was 26,000 and this was expected to grow to about 90,000 by the beginning of the twenty-first century.

However Runcorn is certainly not a new town. Indeed it is a very old town. The Romans established a settlement on Halton Brow in the third century AD. The Normans built a castle on Halton Hill in 1071 and in the twelfth century an Augustinian priory was founded in Runcorn. This was then re-established in Norton in 1133.

The first mention of the hamlet of Runcofan occurs in the Anglo- Saxon Chronicle where it is recorded that in 914 King Alfred's daughter, Ethelfreda built a fortress at the narrows of Runcorn Gap in order to prevent Viking longships from passing up river. This reference pre-dates the foundation of Liverpool by three hundred years!

Runcorn's rise to prominence occurred during the Industrial Revolution in the eighteenth century when it became a vital centre of communications on the inland waterways system. It was by way of the Bridgewater Canal and the Trent and Mersey Canal that Manchester and the Potteries obtained their raw materials and it was via the canals and the port of Runcorn that the finished products of Manchester and Stoke reached a world market.

In Regency times Runcorn was a spa town, an attractive spot to which invalids and pleasure parties came to enjoy the pure air and the salt bathing. However by Victoria's reign the town had become a sooty little industrial centre noted for the manufacture of soap and chemicals and the beginnings of the tanning industry were being established.

In spite of poor communications to the north, Runcorn dominated mid - Merseyside. Widnes was then entirely rural. During the 1840s maritime trade at the small port of Runcorn grew substantially and in order to accommodate the increase in traffic new docks were constructed. In 1847 Runcorn's growing importance was recognised when it was designated a customs port independent of the port of Liverpool. In keeping with its enhanced status a new custom house was built in Old Coach Road.

By the end of the century Runcorn had become a thriving shallow draught port with its quays crowded with schooners bringing the materials required by the pottery, chemical and tanning industries. A vast barge traffic also developed on the upper river as trains of barges were towed to and from Liverpool. Runcorn had a role to play in Liverpool's success for the early industries in the city depended upon Cheshire rock salt which was carried on the Mersey and Weaver rivers and which was refined in Liverpool to be carried to ports all over the world.

During the two world wars Runcorn's industries worked at full capacity providing the chemicals required for munitions. The tanneries also experienced an extraordinary demand for leather and the war years marked the zenith of their commercial success. After the war three events occurred, which changed the appearance of old Runcorn. The first was the redevelopment of the shopping precinct in Church Street and the clearance of old properties in the area. Then came the demolition of housing to make way for New Town building and finally the construction of roads to the new road bridge cut a wide swathe through the town's Mersey ward.

The new bridge has had a great impact on the social and economic life of the region and within ten years it was carrying forty times the traffic carried by the old transporter bridge. Runcorn was no longer a cul-de- sac. Centuries of isolation were at an end and the fields of Cheshire had become within the reach of north Merseyside.

Local industry has been much changed. The sandstone quarries are long gone; the four tanneries have been demolished. There is no commercial traffic on the inland waterways and very little on the Manchester Ship Canal. The local chemical industry is also shrinking.

However, Runcorn is today a much greener place. The industrial grime of a century has been removed from the sandstone churches. The riverfront has been attractively landscaped and old factory sites have been redeveloped.

Runcorn now has a fine new hospital, a large shopping complex, a first class library and a second railway station. It is a place of vigorous industrial and commercial enterprise and the future points to further expansion and success.

Runcorn may be a New Town but it is also and old town with a long history.

Pre-industrial Runcorn.

"The shore all the way to Weston Point is protected by a low ridge of rock rising almost perpendicular from the beach. The lovers of botany may find a pleasing variety of plants, both maritime and inland varieties in the vicinity of this place." John Aikin 1795.

The photo caption says " To Sir R Brooks , Bart. of Norton Priory, This view of Runcorn , is humbly inscibed by his obedient servant, T.Troughton.

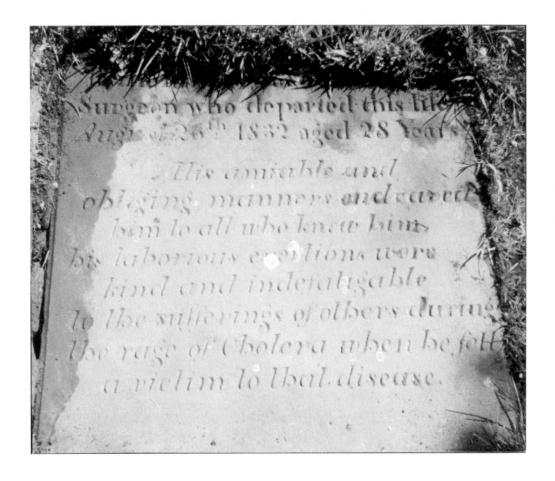

...Surgeon who departed this life
August 26th 1832 aged 28 Years

His amiable and
obliging manners endeared
him to all who knew him
his laborious exertions were
kind and indefatigable
to the sufferings of others during
the rage of Cholera when he fell
a victim to that disease.

In the summer of 1832 cholera was identified in areas of poor housing off Mersey Street. There were 36 cases of the disease and 18 deaths. Cholera claimed John Dunn the surgeon. His gravestone is to be found in All Saints churchyard.

CONTENTS

One   The Bridges   13

Two   Maritime Runcorn   27

Three   Industrial Runcorn   49

Four   Town and Country Views   61

Five   Buildings   77

Six   Church Activity   93

Seven   Pageants and Processions   107

Eight   Some Runcorn Folk   135

A View from the Bridge.

As close as we can get to an aerial photograph without flying.
This spectacular picture taken during construction of the Silver Jubilee bridge
is just one of the many unique photographs included in this book.

One

The Bridges

By 1945 the transporter bridge was hopelessly inadequate. The volume of traffic had increased far beyond its capacity and long queues formed on both sides of the river. Demands for a permanent bridge were finally accepted and in 1956 a start was made on the concrete piers on both sides of the river. Here an ICI minibus is used to transport bridge passengers travelling to Castners or Rocksavage works. The photograph was taken in 1960.

The main span of the transporter bridge was 1000 feet, whilst the towers were 180 feet high. It was the largest transporter bridge ever built and was in operation for fifty-six years from 1905-1961.

The footpath of the railway bridge was essential to communications when the transporter bridge was closed for repair. Hundreds of people relied on the walkway when the transporter was closed for some months in the 1950s.

The demolition of the transporter bridge is well underway in this photograph of 1962. The task took two yeas to complete and today no vestige of this famous structure remains.

The demolition cost was greater than the construction costs of fifty years earlier.

The new Mersey road bridge required the demolition of many well maintained homes in Runcorn. Here work has begun to clear houses which were in the path of the bridge and its approach roads.

The transporter bridge platform could carry twelve cars and over 200 foot passengers. The crossing took about 2½ minutes. The service did not operate after midnight.

Early days in the construction of the new road bridge. The concrete pier has been built in the river bed. Work on the bridge began in 1956.

Assisted by tugs, a large vessel, a Shell Tanker, passes Richard Abel's boat building yard before manoeuvring round the canal bend to the west of the railway bridge.

The arch of the new Mersey road bridge is nearing completion. Princess Alexandra opened the bridge in 1961

The transporter car is about to cross the river as a girder is hoisted into position on the new bridge.

Contractors hoist a girder to complete the arch of the bridge. A workman straddles the gap as the two sections are about to be joined together

A girder is about to be lifted into position from a pontoon in the Manchester Ship Canal.

On Monday 14th November 1960 the creeper cranes lowered the last steel sections into place. The operation took thirty hours of patient work before the half arches were levered together and the 6000 tons of steel girders were locked into position.

The new bridge dwarfs the railway bridge. At the top of the photograph can be seen West Bank power station in Widnes, since demolished. West Bank Dock was filled in when river traffic ceased in the 1970s.

All in a day's work. Hair raising feats as workmen stroll on the girders of the Bridge nearly 300 feet over the river.

Muffled against the cold November weather the bridge contractors inspect the work as the topmost girders of the arch are fitted into place.

A workman nonchalantly surveys work on the new bridge from a precarious position above West Bank power station and West Bank Dock in Widnes

Not all it seems. The camera angle has created the illusion that the transporter bridge car has become entangled with the new bridge works..

Here the deck of the new bridge is nearing completion, the elegant arch contrasts vividly with the stark masonry of the railway bridge which was built ninety-three years previously.

The opening of the Mersey Road Bridge in 1961. Amongst the prominent townsfolk are Councillors Robin Gray, George Povey and George Dutton as well as Denis Vosper MP and Mrs Vosper.

Princess Alexandra at the opening ceremony on July 21st 1961. The new toll-free bridge took five years to construct at a cost of £3 million with another £1.5 million for the approach roads. The bridge made an instant impact on the social and economic life of the region, for improved communications made possible the development of Runcorn New Town. The bridge was widened and renamed the 'Silver Jubilee Bridge' by the Rt Hon William Rogers M.P on 28th October 1977.

Two

Maritime
Runcorn

The Old Quay Canal or the Runcorn to Latchford Canal of the Mersey and Irwell Navigation Company is nearing the end of its useful days in this photograph. After supplying much of the building material for the construction of Salford Docks, the canal was swept away during the building of the Manchester Ship Canal.

The piles are in position prior to the constructions of the Ship Canal sea wall (known locally as the gantry wall). The photograph was taken in 1890.

PARISH CHURCH   RUNCORN

The Runcorn waterfront before the building of the transporter bridge, about 1895.

Runcorn docks crowded with sailing vessels about 1905. The town remained a sailing ship port until the very last days of sail just before the Second World War..

The barquentine *Waterwitch* was built in Poole in 1871. She was one of the larger sailing vessels to use the port of Runcorn. '*Waterwitch*' was the last square rigged sailing ship registered in Britain to carry cargo for a living. She made her last voyage with coal from the Mersey to Falmouth in 1936 and was then sold to Estonian owners.

Sailing vessels, barges and narrowboats are seen in Runcorn docks at the end of the nineteenth century.

A scene at Runcorn Docks before the First World War. Until the mid 1930s the docks were crowded with schooners which brought potters' materials from Devon and Cornwall.

This photograph was taken before the Manchester Ship Canal was built. Runcorn was then a sailing ship port and steam vessels were in the minority.

The Bridgewater Canal was still a busy waterway in the early years of the twentieth century. A suggested date for this photograph is 1905.

Top Locks in the 1930s. The railways and mechanised road transport brought about a rapid decline in traffic on the Bridgewater Canal during the early decades of the twentieth century. The famous lines of locks were demolished and filled in when the new roads to the road bridge were being built in 1960.

Weston Point docks showing piles of pottery material awaiting transport on to Stoke-on-Trent. This traffic was soon to end and this picture of the late 1940s shows that the only boats to be seen are pleasure craft.

Two working narrowboats pass up the locks in the 1950s.

A narrow beam tug is seen under Waterloo Bridge. At one time there were twenty-six narrow beam tugs operating on the Bridgewater and Trent and Mersey canals.

Unloading bags of sugar at the Runcorn town warehouse circa 1920.

The barge *Carrier* is launched in 1911 from the Sprinch boat building yard in Victoria Road. The yard was reputed to be the best equipped boatyard in the country. Hundreds of Bridgewater craft were repaired there.

Of the twenty-six narrow beam tugs used by the Bridgewater Navigation Company only *Runcorn* (above) built in 1874 was constructed of wood. She is seen at Top Locks in the 1930s.

Unloading bags of phosphates from the motor vessel *Audacia* into a barge circa 1960.

Weston Point docks seen during the 1960s. Christ Church became redundant in the 1990s.

Old Quay yard was a busy place in the early 1960s when this photograph was taken.

The quayside buildings of the Mersey and Irwell Navigation Company go back to 1804. The Mersey and Irwell's Old Quay Canal became a serious rival to the Duke of Bridgewater's undertaking. The waterways were combined in 1844 and both were purchased by the Manchester Ship Canal Company in 1885.

At the beginning of the 21st century Old Quay Yard has been transformed with an area of high rise apartments which command extensive views across the Mersey.

The Top Locks in the 1920s. The old line of locks was closed in 1949 and the new line in 1960. Both have been filled in so that today the Bridgewater Canal has no exit to the Manchester Ship Canal.

After the war, in an attempt to win business Runcorn docks were modernised. Here modern cactus grabs are being used to discharge cargoes.

Sailing flats seen in Weston Point docks in 1930. These shallow draught vessels were built specifically for operating in the difficult conditions in the River Mersey and River Weaver.

The early Runcorn industries were sited on the inland waterways. All the tanneries received their hides and raw materials via the canals. Here a barge is seen moored alongside Highfield Tannery.

The Upper Mersey Navigation Company's wooden buoying tender *Preston* was built in Brundrit and Whiteways' Mersey Street shipyard in 1867. She was employed in the task of plotting the river's navigable channel until replaced by the *Lady Windsor* in 1922.

In the 19th and 20th centuries there were scores of fishing smacks registered at the Port of Runcorn. The little craft ventured off the mouth of the river Dee and off the Lancashire coast to land their catches of shrimps at Old Quay. This photograph was probably taken in the 1930s.

For ten years the buoy laying vessel *Lady Windsor* was used by the Upper Mersey Commissioners to mark the river's sailing channels. The boat was also used to supply the lightships and the lighthouse at Hale Head. This vessel was replaced by *Jesse Wallwork* in 1932. The river is no longer buoyed for today there is no commercial traffic on the Upper Mersey.

Assisted by tugs, the steamer *Manipur* passes under the transporter bridge. The photograph is believed to have been taken in the late 1930s. Children can be seen diving into the canal from the bridge fenders.

The Irish coaster *Carrigrennan* carrying a cargo of soda ash from Northwich to Dublin is seen on the River Weaver about 1960.

Throughout the 18th and 19th centuries the River Weaver was a vital waterway with hundreds of sailing flats engaged in carrying rock salt to the refineries in Liverpool. The ICI company operated small steamers like this one working between Northwich and Liverpool and Birkenhead docks.

Ships tied up at the wall to the east of the transporter bridge were once a familiar sight when the Ship Canal was a busy waterway. Here *Cinulia* awaits the tugs which will convey her to Eastham.

The 'Duker' paddle tug *Dagmar* was built in 1863. She was one of half a dozen similar boats which were employed in towing on the upper Mersey. *Dagmar* reached the venerable age of sixty-three years before she went to the breaker's yard in 1926.

Until a few years ago there was a thriving export trade in scrap iron from Weston Point docks. This scene is Delamere Dock about 1980.

When business was booming in the 1950s there were 26 traffic tugs in service on the Manchester Ship Canal as well as a number of small tugs employed by the Company's dredging department.

The company's first tugs were paddle boats which were inherited from the Bridgewater Navigation Company and which had been used on the upper River Mersey before the canal was built.

Here the paddle tug *Rixton* is seen at Runcorn.

With the decline of the inland waterways narrowboats were abandoned in backwaters. This boat still retains the plank by which it was 'legged' through the narrow tunnels on the Trent and Mersey Canal. The leggers worked the boat along by literally walking on the tunnel sides, while the horse would be walked over the top of the tunnel to meet the boat at the other end.

Bearing the impressive RN registration letters for the port of Runcorn, a fishing smack is photographed at high tide at Old Quay.

The most modern Ship Canal tugs were built in the late 1950s. *Sceptre* was purchased in 1956.

Three

Industrial Runcorn

Quarrying was the first of Runcorn's industries. From the early nineteenth century the Runcorn and Weston sandstone was used over a wide area of the north west of the country. By 1830 soap making had become all important and a few years later the soapworks began to manufacture basic chemicals. Later in the century the town became noted as the most important centre for leather production in the country.

By 1900 the quarries were being worked out and before the First World War the soap works had also closed. The tanneries flourished until just after the Second World War when substitutes for leather brought an end to the local industry. Chemical manufacture still remains important but production is much reduced (Above) Tipping coal slack from waggons at Weston Point power station in about 1920.

Members of the workforce at Ockleston's Halton Road tannery circa 1920.

A rare sight, this shows the reservoir at Runcorn Hill being drained for maintenance and repairs. The local waterworks began operations in March 1868 when water was pumped into a covered reservoir on Beacon Hill. An efficient water supply was essential for Runcorn's tanning and chemical industries.

Highfield Tannery showing damage caused by a fire in the 1890s. Of the town's four tanneries Highfield was the last to close. Production ceased in 1968.

An inscription on the back of this photograph tells us that this steam lorry was *"delivered in June 1922 and the driver was Harry Crompton, the foreman at Bankes' Lane Garage."* In 1890 48 chemical firms including 14 from Widnes and 3 from Runcorn, combined to form the huge United Alkali Company.

Evans, Lescher and Webb Ltd established a medical research laboratory in Runcorn in the early years of the 20th century. The firm produced anti-toxins, sera and vaccines as well as synthetic pharmaceutical drugs. The firm ceased production after the Second World War and the factory was demolished.

A steam lorry and half a dozen motor cars make up Castner Kellner's transport fleet. The photograph was taken circa 1910.

The gas engine operated Old Quay Swing Bridge on the Manchester Ship Canal. It was installed in 1893.

Castner Kellner's factory included a power station in order to supply electricity for the large scale decomposition of brine. The photograph shows work on the construction of the power station circa 1910.

ICI's Weston Point Power station nears completion.

A lorry with solid tyres laden with carboys of acid. The photograph is said to have been taken at Wigg's works circa 1920.

Boston's Puritan Tannery in Halton Road was the most modern of the local tanneries. At one time the famous Puritan advertisement could be seen on most of the country's railway stations. From 1958 man-made synthetic substitutes for leather brought about the closure of the four Runcorn tanneries within a decade.

The workforce of Runcorn Gas Company in a photograph taken at the Halton Road site in 1938. The Runcorn Gas Company was incorporated in 1837 on a site which later became Gas Street in the centre of the town. The gas works was later relocated in Halton Road. Today the site is derelict awaiting redevelopment.

Runcorn railway station has been much changed since this picture was taken in 1960. The railway sidings and the goods office have been cleared away to make a vast car park and the station buildings have been modernised.

The busy railway sidings at Runcorn station a few years before the car park development.

Castner Kellner's fire brigades and the first aid teams were always highly successful in inter-works competitions. Here at Blackpool in 1949 they achieved first place in pump drill and first place for ambulance service.

209778 J.V.

View from Alton Castle, Run

Industrial mid Merseyside in the early 1930's. Widnes dominated the scene with scores of factory chimneys whereas south of the river there were still farm fields between Halton and Runcorn.

Four

Town and Country Views

Writing before work on the New Town has started, Nikolaus Pevsner, the famous architectural historian said: "*Halton village on its rock is still a village. Soon it will be New Runcorn and may the planners fully realise what a visual treasure they have in this rock.*"

This photograph captures the rural peace of Halton village before the advent of the New Town. The views from the hill were spectacular - a patchwork of small fields of barley, potatoes and pasture which extended to the horizon.

Sad to say many attractive prospects like the one illustrated here disappeared forever behind the new buildings.

This view of Halton was taken before 1913 when a fall of masonry much reduced the ruins of the castle. Top right is Hill School which was demolished about forty years ago. The reapers are seen on the old field path which linked Halton village to Halton Brook.

From the late 1960s the countryside surrounding Halton began to disappear as new estates were built. Thirty-seven farms and 7500 acres of farmland were taken to complete the New Town.

Heath Road, Weston Village in 1909. The industrialisation of Weston Point in Victorian times brought about the expansion of Weston Village to accommodate the workers from the new factories. Like many similar properties in the town Heath Road houses have now been transformed by cement rendering and colour washing.

Today Moughland Lane is one of the busiest roads in the town. In 1944 it was as quiet as a country lane.

An agricultural thresher and a baling machine broke loose from the traction engine which was towing them over Delph Bridge in 1925. Fortunately no one was injured.

Women and girls search for coal in the Bridgewater Canal which has been drained for repairs. The coal had fallen from barges which had been unloaded at Runcorn and Weston Alkali Works. Runcorn Town Bridge (Savage's Bridge) can be seen. Suggested date 1895

Domestic refuse collection in Runcorn in the 1920s. Here a Sentinel steam tipper lorry is at work.

Until the advent of the New Town, Halton village was a detached farming community. A suggested date for this photograph of Grice's farm is 1960.

Before the days of motor traffic every village had its smithy. The picture is of Sutton Weaver smithy in Station Road.

The little shop in Bridge Street at Delph Bridge later became well known as Mrs Richardson's café. All the shops in Bridge Street were pulled down about thirty years ago.

A leisurely pony and trap seems to arouse curiosity in High Street in the early years of the twentieth century.

Looking down Bridge Street from Delph Bridge. Nothing seen here survived the redevelopment carried out a few years ago.

Lowlands Road looking towards the railway station before redevelopment took place for the construction of roads to the new road bridge. Today nothing remains of the scene pictured here.

The new Mersey Road is seen under construction in 1924. The improvement was made possible when the Manchester Ship Canal company provided a strip of land to allow the widening of the old road. The construction provided work for many during a period of acute unemployment.

The new Mersey Road was opened on March 20th 1924 by Ernest Latimer, the Managing Director of the Manchester Ship Canal Company. Also seen in the photograph are Alfred Grounds, Chairman of the Runcorn Urban District Council and James Wilding, Surveyor to the Council.

In 1950 a double decker bus passes through the quiet Main Street of Halton village. Today the density of traffic and street parking make it difficult for large vehicles to pass one another in the narrow street.

Up until the 1970s Halton village was a detached community of a few hundred inhabitants. Something of its isolation can be seen in this view of Lodge Lane. Halton Lea Shopping precinct now occupies the site.

Walker's Garage on Savages' Bridge was a familiar landmark until it was demolished to make way for the roads to the new bridge.

The Primitive Methodist chapel with its Sunday school in Greenway Road was built in 1871. They were demolished to make way for new roads to the bridge.

Runcorn AFC's Canal Street ground presents a worn surface at the end of the playing season. Soon the ground would be sold for housing and the team would not have a home in Runcorn. The Linnets are now forced to play their 'home' games a dozen miles out of town in Northwich.

A view of Ellesmere Street with the Commercial Hotel (usually known as the Glass Barrel) seen from the market. The area was redeveloped about thirty years ago.

The Market Hall and the Bus Station were part of post war development in the old town centre. The scene has changed in the last few years with the construction of a new market and busway bus station.

The three bridges viewed from the east in 1960. Both Halton Road and Canal Street are free of traffic. New Town development has resulted in considerable changes to this scene. New houses now occupy the site of Runcorn Football Club

A view from the gantry wall taken as the bridge arch nears completion.

Five

Buildings

During the Middle Ages there was a moated house in the deer park at Halton. Hallwood was the home of the Chesshyre family. Sir John Chesshyre was born in the house in 1662. He was called to the bar in 1689 and by 1727 he was knighted and was appointed His Majesty's Premier Sergeant at Law. Hallwood house was much altered over the years. Its very fine south facing classical façade had to be demolished after becoming unsafe due to bombing during the war. Hallwood has been modernised to become the Tricorn public house.

In the 1860's when Runcorn had become an established port of some importance, the Camden Buildings were constructed in the High Street to house prestigious shops in the middle of the old town.
Sadly today the buildings are almost derelict.

The Panorama Hotel, formerly the Manor Residential Hotel in Castle Road, Halton, dominates the village street. This impressive Victorian house was at the time of writing empty and boarded up. An application has been made for the building of 14 apartments on the site.

In the nineteenth century practically every street had a beer house. The Lancers Inn in Wellington Street dates from about 1850. It was renamed to become the Oddfellows and closed as a public house over thirty years ago.

An eighteenth century form of refrigeration, which only the very rich could afford. The ice house at Norton Priory.

It is hard to believe that the Bridge Hotel in Ashridge Street was at one time the headquarters of the local bowling league. The green was said to be the best in the town. The hotel was demolished in the late 1950s.

The Technical Institute was built in Waterloo Road in 1894 by public subscription. Sir John Brunner was a generous benefactor. He also gave money to equip the laboratories. The building served a dual role from 1902 when it accommodated pupils of the new Runcorn County Secondary School (Grammar). The building has been empty for some time and may soon be demolished.

The South Bank Hotel was once the home of the town's first industrialist, Dennis Brundrit. He built his new gothic mansion about 1845. It was set in gardens and an orchard on a country lane leading to the ferry crossing. The South Bank is awaiting redevelopment.

Halton Lodge Farm, known locally as Grice's farm was built by Charles Wigg the industrialist. Halton Lodge Primary School now occupies the site.

Today all that remains of Halton Lodge are the gateposts which have been re-erected in the grounds of Halton Lodge primary school.

It is many years since a drink was served in the Lord Rodney in Church Street. The old inn is now a chip shop.

The Egerton Arms in Irwell Lane was one of the oldest public houses in Runcorn. It was demolished in 2006.

In 1906 Runcorn's market hall which was built in 1856 was adapted to make the town's swimming pool. The outdoor market is seen here.

The La Scala formerly the Palace in High Street was one of three Runcorn cinemas. The site is awaiting redevelopment.

These attractive cottages in Castle Road, Halton were believed to have been built for quarry workers in the early eighteenth century.

Originally a workshop for a shipyard this building was for many years known as T.S *Ashanti*, the headquarters of the local sea cadets.

Runcorn's Town Warehouse at Top Locks was built in the early years of the nineteenth century. It was used by the Cooperative Wholesale Society to ship flour and sugar from Liverpool. The building is now derelict and awaiting demolition.

The Cleveland Hotel in Greenway Road was a casualty of the clearances which took place nearly fifty years ago when the road bridge was being built.

The Man at the Wheel, at the corner of Church Street and Granville Street was closed in 1926. It is now the premises of an estate agent.

The Mariners Hotel in Perceval Lane was pulled down many years ago.

The Seneschal's House was built in 1598. Until fairly recent times it was known as the Brow Farm.

Georgian elegance. St Mary's Vicarage and Sir John Chesshyre's library in Castle Road, Halton. The library was built in 1733 and the vicarage a few years later.

The Old Hall on Halton Common bears a plaque stating that it was rebuilt in 1693. It is believed that that house was reduced to a ruin during the Civil War fifty years earlier.

In Halton village there are many period buildings including Elizabethan, Jacobean, Georgian and Victorian houses. This seventeenth century house in Main Street was formerly known as the Village Farm.

Aston Hall was built by Sir Willoughby Aston in 1668. In 1793 it was remodelled by Samuel Wyatt, the famous architect. At the same time the grounds were landscaped by Humphrey Repton who succeeded Capability Brown as Britain's most notable landscape gardener. Aston Hall was pulled down in 1938. The illustration is a watercolour of about 1810.

Six

Church
Activity

Watercolour of the medieval parish church as seen from Church Lane showing
the 1802 rebuilding of the south side.

All Saints Parish School in Church Street is the oldest school in Runcorn. It dates back to 1811. By 1914 a new school had been planned and in that year the foundation stone was laid. However, because of wartime conditions and mounting costs after the war, the school was never built. It was not until 1977 that the new All Saints Primary School was built on an adjacent site. The photograph was taken at the foundation stone ceremony in 1914.

This photograph of the happy choir of St John's Church, Weston Village was taken in the early 1970s. The vicar is the Reverend Gordon Roxby.

Holy Trinity Sunday School's May Queen, Jeanette Felicity leads the procession in High Street.

In 1858 a Sunday School was opened for the children of local Methodists in a cottage in Gilbert Street. The success of the venture resulted in the formation of the Camden Society and the building of Camden Chapel in Lowlands Road in 1863.

Camden Chapel was the first of Runcorn's Methodist churches. It was built by Thomas Hazlehurst, the soap manufacturer in 1862. It was pulled down for the new Mersey road bridge and road works in the 1960s.

Parishioners enjoy a tea party on the lawn of the old vicarage in Highland's Road in 1908.

Camden Methodist Sunday School scholars are seen in Greenway Road in the Whitsuntide procession of 1968.

The Whit processions were always well attended by both participants and by spectators. A suggested date for this occasion is 1912.

The steeple of Runcorn's All Saints Parish church is 161 feet in height. Originally it was topped by a weather vane. This has not been seen for many years. The photograph shows the removal of the weather cock in 1926.

At one time every church in Runcorn boasted a fully robed choir. In the 1930s St John's in Weston village had an all male choir.

Ensign E.A Fletcher and Lieutenant E.E Brennan of the Runcorn Salvation Army in a photograph taken in May 1920. For many years the Citadel or headquarters of the Salvation Army was a prominent feature in High Street.

A large crowd attends the Armistice Day service at the war memorial in Moughland Lane in the early 1930s.

Some appreciation of the enthusiasm for the Whit Walk processions can be seen in the numbers attending this walk in the 1950s.

The vicar of Runcorn, Archdeacon Alfred Wood and his wife are seen outside the old Georgian vicarage in Highlands Road about 1908. Archdeacon Wood was the vicar of Runcorn from 1887 to 1911. He died in 1918.

Proudly wearing their medals, a large crowd of ex soldiers attend the service at the war memorial in Greenway Road in the 1920s.

St Luke's Congregational Chapel in Mason Street. Harvest service in the 1930s. In the pulpit Miss Edna Gibbons, left to right Miss F Dutton, Walter Bennett, Jack Wilkinson, J. Bennett, Miss G Buckley, Miss C Wilkinson. The chapel was demolished to make way for the New Town development with the last service being held in April 1968.

Catholic clergy accompany St Edward's schoolchildren on a trip to Frodsham Hill in the early 1930s. The famous helter-skelter can be seen in the background.

Holy Trinity schoolchildren assemble outside the church in Pool Lane, before taking part in the annual Whit Walk.

The framework of the new St Edwards church in Ivy Street is under
construction in 1955.

Halton Village Fete...crowning Rose Queen c 1950.

The Victoria Memorial Hospital, known locally as the Cottage Hospital was opened in 1903 and over the following twenty years it was enlarged to provide the town with a much needed amenity. The Cottage Hospital relied on the generous financial support of the Runcorn public. After the First World War, in order to raise funds for the hospital, the Runcorn Council sponsored the Runcorn Festival or Carnival, a well organised pageant and procession which involved the schools, local industry and the leading personalities of the town. The various tableaux paraded through the town accompanied by brass bands, the organised youth movements and the Fire Brigade, it was the spectacle of the year. The vast procession made its way to the Canal Street football ground where there were refreshments and side shows.

Above - Watched by many sightseers the dancers provide entertainment at the Runcorn Carnival in the 1920s.

The annual Runcorn Carnival was a highly organised event with much care and pride given to costume design. The photograph was taken at the carnival of 1924.

An example of the painstaking attention to costume detail. Eighteenth century youngsters in the Runcorn Carnival c 1924.

Festival frolics. The dancers attracted an appreciative audience at the Runcorn Carnival of 1924.

Carnival capers. The participants are seen in Ashridge Street about 1935.

Toy soldiers are on parade at the Runcorn Carnival in the early 1920s.

The annual Runcorn Festival or Carnival. This event attracted spectators from outlying areas. Many came from Widnes to enjoy the spectacle.

A charming group of young ladies present their tableau extolling the blessings of peace in the world.

The Whit Walk passes over Doctors Bridge c 1922.

Halton British Legion's Fete was a highly organised and well attended occasion. Here the dancers are seen in the village Main street c 1950.

The annual village Rose Fetes provided much pleasure and excitement for many children. Sadly they are now traditions that are in the past.

Mrs H Gamon has crowned Sheila Wyche at the Halton Rose Fete in 1948. Barbara Basnett is the Lady in Waiting.

The lasses of Halton village are pictured at a United Nations ceremony about 1960

A guard of honour salutes the Rose Queen at the Halton village fete in the 1950s.

Halton Rose Fete was always well attended and its demise has been much regretted by local folk.

In the Halton British Legion Rose Fete of 1949 the Rose Queen was Lilian Sutton whilst the ex Queen was Sheila Wyche.

Junior participants in Halton British Legion fete pose for their photograph at Spark Lane

A scene in Halton village Main Street as the dancers proceed to the fair ground celebrations at the village fete in the early 1950s.

Fairground roundabouts helped to make the Halton annual Rose Fete a memorable occasion.

The ceremony of the Rose Queen at Halton village fete c 1950.

A happy group of participants in the Halton Rose Fete of 1950.

The Rose Fetes were always happy occasions. They ceased with the increase in traffic. The tableaux and the processions could not pass through the narrow village streets.

Spectators at Halton British Legion Rose Fete pose for a photograph c 1950.

Ladies taking part in the Whit Walk are seen in front of the Cleveland Hotel in Greenway Road about 1908.

A ladies group in a Whit Walk during the 1950s

The Freedom of the Borough of Halton is awarded to the 22nd (Cheshire)
Regiment on 13th July 1989. The regiment is seen turning from Church Street
into High Street. In September 2007 the Cheshire Regiment was amalgamated
with two neighbouring regiments to form the Mercian Regiment.

Halton's annual village fete was a notable occasion. It always attracted a large crowd of young and old. Fairground amusements added to the carnival atmosphere. This photograph was taken in 1948.

about 1900

The inscription on the drum reads: Weston Brass Band 1880

A hundred years ago Weston boasted two brass bands. This is Weston village brass band about 1900.

Weston Wesleyan Brass Band taken some time in the early 1920s. Back row: F. Kirkham, F. Leach, A. Evans, W. Ward, A. Roberts, nson, H. Baker, S. Spruce, J. Leach. Middle row: H. Bates, W. Hope, E. Bradley, W. Tudor (leader), E. Griffiths, B. Kirkham, A. D Astbury. Front row: H. Bell, ?, J. Griffiths, G. Molyneux.

Brass bands and drum and fife bands were popular in many churches during the nineteenth century. Here the Weston Wesleyan brass band is seen in the early 1920s.

125

The first decade of the twentieth century saw the beginning of the Boy Scout movement. The photograph was taken about 1908.

A wedding party pose for a photograph on the bowling green of the Bridge Inn in Ashridge Street in 1910.

Wedding guests in formal pose in another photograph taken on the bowling green at the Bridge Inn in Ashridge Street in 1927.

Runcorn once boasted successful water polo teams which attracted considerable support. This photograph was probably taken about 1920.

An historic event at Runcorn swimming baths, when in 1929 mixed bathing was permitted for the first time. The notice warns bathers that "Diving from the gallery is strictly prohibited".

A day trip to the seaside sets off from the Bridge Inn in Ashridge Street in the late 1920s.

Once a familiar sight, boys diving off the Gantry wall into the Manchester
Ship Canal at Old Quay in the 1930s.

A street party in Dukes Fields to celebrate VE Day in 1945.

A street party to celebrate the coronation of George VI and Queen Elizabeth in 1937.

Television personality Pat Phoenix (Elsie Tanner of Coronation Street) is the guest of the Runcorn Darts League. L to R Councillor Robin Gray; Pat Phoenix; Bill Horsefield, the licensee of the Halfway House and George Newby, Secretary of the Runcorn Darts League

A social function takes place at the Wilsons Hotel in 1944.

The undated placard reads "Runcorn White Star RFC Lancashire Junior Cup and Medals".

In the early years of the nineteenth century the Wilsons Hotel was known as the Bowling Green Inn. For many years now the hotel's bowling green has been a car park. This photograph shows the Wilsons' bowling enthusiasts c 1920

Enthusiastic anglers rescue fish in the Big Pool before it was built over to make roads for the new Mersey road bridge. The fish were released into the Bridgewater Canal. The photograph was taken in July 1960.

After enjoying a spell in the swimming baths the children usually made their way across Bridge Street to sample the delights of Carlisle's (formerly Stubbs') sweet shop.

Runcorn Athletic AFC. Winners of the Cheshire Amateur League Championship in 1962. Players: second row L to R Ted Collins, Russ Bradbury, Roy Simpson, Ralph Wilkinson, Billy Hough, Roy Cox. Front row John Thompson, Tony Ireland, Stan Furnival, Wilf Jones, Bill Hoxworth, Tony Redican.

Eight

Some Runcorn Folk

An Edwardian wedding. A hundred years ago in September 1908, Frank Johnson and Mary Brimelow were married in Halton Road Methodist Church. The bridesmaids were two sisters of the bride and the groom's sister.

On December 7th 1916 a banquet was given at the Exchange Station Hotel in Liverpool to celebrate the centenary of Hazlehurst and Sons Ltd. Hazlehursts was acquired from the United Alkali Company by Levers who closed the soapworks in 1913 and transferred production to Port Sunlight. Among the 150 guests were some retired employees of the firm. Hazlehursts' brand name was still in use in the 1930s.

A unique institution. In 1903 the Runcorn Grappling Corps was formed. A hundred years ago the canals were busy and drowning was a remarkably frequent occurrence. The corps was often called upon to recover bodies from the town's waterways. The volunteer corps members are; Back row L to R; unidentified; Jim Capewell; Superintendent Thomas Atherton; Harold Farmer; Tom Nicholls. Front row; Tom Griffiths; Bill Martin; unidentified; Jack Bellfield; Herbert Pickstock.

The boys of Runcorn County Secondary School (Better known as Balfour Road School) are seen in formal pose in 1927.

The sixth form at the Runcorn County Grammar School seen at the Waterloo Road site in 1946. Within a couple of years the school was closed and the pupils were transferred to Helsby Grammar School.

Runcorn was the birthplace of a famous Victorian novelist and dramatist, Thomas Henry Hall Caine, born in Bridgewater Street in 1853. He was a friend of Dante Gabrielle Rossetti who encouraged him to write romantic novels. These were very popular with *The Deemster* of 1887, *The Manxman* of 1884 and *The Eternal City* of 1901 being the best known. Caine also wrote *Recollections of Rossetti*. He was also a friend of Bram Stoker who wrote *Dracula*. Of Manx blood on his father's side, Caine lived in the Isle of Man where he was a member of the House of Keys. He was knighted in 1918 and made a Companion of Honour in 1922. He died in 1931. He is pictured here with his wife, Mary, and his son, Ralph in 1895.

The dinner celebrating the centenary of the *Runcorn Guardian* at the Waterloo Hotel in April 1962. Among the guests were J.E Armitage, Managing Director of Mackie and Co, Shaun Lambert, Manager *Runcorn Guardian* and Terry Magee, chief reporter. The newspaper ceased publication in 1980

The War memorial in Moughland Lane was unveiled in November 1920. Seen here are the Chairman of the Council, Mr R.H Posnett and Major G Ashton who is about to lay the first wreath. An estimated 10,000 people attended the ceremony.

Halton village football team on the field in Spark Lane in the 1950s. Back row L to R; M Phillipson; G Rowe; H Tomlinson, B Dunbebin, R Newton, B Marshall. Front row; Ron Ellis, A Ocego, Ray Ellis, A Bold, H Bell.

Staff of Balfour Road Boys School, Runcorn, late 1950s. Back row L to R unidentified; Jim Chadwick, Eric Walters; Bill Cooke; Frank Fursland; Charles Jenner; John Smith; John Tavlin. Front row unidentified; Eric Jones; Herbert Thomas (Headmaster from 1960); Len Jones (Headmaster until 1960); Wilf Riding; W.E Hartles; Eric Harrison.

Clifton (Rocksavage) Methodist Chapel Sunday School prize giving in the 1950s. The chapel was closed about fifty years ago.

Camden Methodist Chapel amateur dramatic society present the musical play 'A Village Wedding' about 1960.

MORE GREAT BOOKS AND DVDS
AVAILABLE DIRECT FROM
MIDDLEVIEW
ALL PRICES INCLUDE P&P IN UK

Middleview, New Road,
GWESPYR
Flintshire, UK.
Tel : 01745 886769
email: info@Middleview.co.uk or
info@AvidPublications.co.uk
website http// www.avidpublications.co.uk
Middleview welcomes new authors

JUST NUISANCE AB - His full story
by Terence Sisson

The amazing but true story of the only dog that was officially enlisted into the British Royal Navy, a Great Dane whose name was Nuisance, his official rank and name was AB Just Nuisance. Famed for his preference for the company of navy ratings (he wasn't too keen on Officers) in and around the famous World War II naval base of Simonstown, South Africa, Nuisance helped many a sailor rejoin his ship after a night on the town.
Today his own statue overlooking the bay off the Cape of Good Hope commemorates AB Just Nuisance.

£10.00

FORGOTTON EMPRESS
- The Tragedy of the Empress of Ireland
- by David Zeni

Tells the fascinating story of the Canadian Pacific Passenger liner *RMS Empress of Ireland*. On her way home to Liverpool from Canada, she was sunk in a collision on the St. Lawrence River. Two years after the *Titanic*, it was, in terms of passenger fatalities, an even greater tragedy. These two ships, along with the *Lusitania*, form a triumvirate of maritime tragedies, all within a three-year period, that sent shock waves around the world.

Yet whilst *Titanic* and *Lusitania* seem to be almost household names, the disaster that befell the *Empress of Ireland* has until now always been shrouded in the cloak of history, as impenetrable as the fog that brought about her total loss, along with 1,012 lives, on 29th May 1914. With a chilling connection to the 'Crippen Murders' and containing never-before-published material, Forgotten Empress grips the reader in such a way it is hard to put aside... a thoroughly excellent book.

'...dubbed 'The 'Forgotten Empress'...the second in a shocking trio of tragedies at sea...sandwiched in between the disasters of the Titanic and the Lusitania, ...it was a sudden death... that sent Liverpool into mourning...'
Liverpool Echo

' Zeni brings a fresh, moment by moment urgency to this real life tragic drama' Winnipeg Free Press

ISBN   978-1-902964-15-7   £14.50

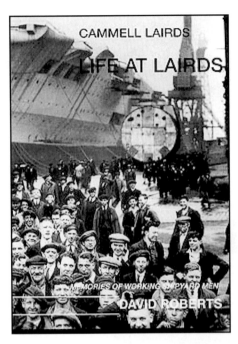

'Life at Lairds - Memories of Working Shipyard Men'
by David Roberts

'The time may not be far off when young people will ask, What did they do there, what were they like? This book answers the questions......'
Sea Breezes

'A book full of anecdotes and rich in humanity...a piece of social History.....'
Liverpool Echo

ISBN   0 9521020 1 3   £9.00

'Cammell Laird - the golden years'
by David Roberts.
With a foreword by Frank Field MP.
'Captures life in the prosperous years at the historic Birkenhead shipyard......' Liverpool Echo

'Puts into perspective ... the strikes... the Polaris contract... and those who worked at the yard...' Sea Breezes

ISBN   0 9521020 2 1   £9.00.

BLUE FUNNEL - VOYAGE EAST
by Award winning author
Richard Woodman

What was life like aboard a British vessel in the last great days of the Merchant Navy? Blue Funnel - Voyage East takes us in one of the Holt Line's 'China Boats' on a typical trip out of the Mersey, to the Far East and back again by way of Suez. The time is the 1960s and it is a style of seafaring now totally lost among today's container ships and roll on - roll off ferries.

We keep the long watches of the night; observe officers and men, sea and weather, in every mood. We learn about the transvestites of Singapore and the almond-eyed whores of Hong Kong, as well as the intricacies of derricks and cargo stowage - human hair and hog bristle from China, liquid latex and palm oil from Malaya. We can puzzle over the mysteries of navigation, what motivates the First Mate and why any sane man should go to sea, far from home and the love of good women. The author draws on his many years service in Blue Funnel cargo liners to capture the sights, smells, enormous satisfactions and aching sadness that attended the 'carriage of general cargo in open stows'.

'This is life at sea, warts and all, and a better book because of it.'..........**Sea Breezes**

ISBN 978-1-902964-04-1   £15.50

CHILDREN OF THE BENARES - by RALPH BARKER

Foreword by Beth Williams (nee Cummings) - the only Liverpool
Survivor.

The Ellerman and City passenger liner *City of Benares* left Liverpool on
Friday 13th September 1940 carrying a precious cargo - 90 children from
the bombed cities of Britain bound for safe haven away from the war - to
Canada.

Four days later, without warning, she was torpedoed and sunk by a
German U-boat in mid - Atlantic. 256 people were lost including, at first
count, 83 of the evacuee children.

An event that shocked the world in its brutality, much use of the atrocity
was made by the British authorities in an attempt to persuade the United
States into joining the conflict.

However it was not long before the parents of the lost children, who had
entrusted their loved ones to the evacuation scheme, began to suspect
those same authorities of neglect, when they learned that the promised
naval escort for the convoy had abandoned the unarmed ships twenty-
one hours before the U-boat struck!

There were allegations of crew rushing the lifeboats, poor equipment and
even racial prejudice in the ensuing clamour for an explanation. Yet
somehow a formal investigation was avoided and the scandal covered up.
Children of the Benares is a gripping story of the disaster itself and
exposes at last what went on behind the scenes at the Ministry of
Shipping and the British Admiralty. It is a chilling tale of fallibility and
human survival.

ISBN 978-1-902964-07-2   £15.50

D V D

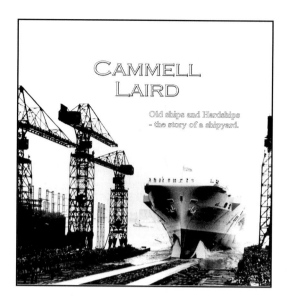

'Cammell Laird, Old Ships and Hardships'
- The Story of a Shipyard.

After an extensive search for moving footage of this world
famous shipyard at work a video of the history of this
shipyard has at last been compiled. How Cammell Laird
served the nation through two World Wars, building world
famous vessels like the Rodney, Hood, Mauritania, Ark Royal,
Windsor Castle and many more, up to the tragic day in 1993
when Lairds was shut down.
The story of the yard is also told through the voices of the
men who worked at Lairds; Welders, Cranedrivers,
Electricians and Plumbers, they tell of the hardships of
building ships in all weathers and the lighter moments that
came from some of the 'characters' of the yard.

'contains rare archive film & photographs that anyone
connected with the the world famous shipyard will remember
and enjoy.'....... Birkenhead News

Running time approx: 56.00 mins -. £17.95

Blue Funnel - *Voyages and Voices*

Blue Funnel
Voyages & Voices

Compiled with the help of never before published film taken all over the world by some of those men who actually sailed with 'Blueys' on many of their well-known vessels.

Contains some of the sights and sounds of typical Blue Funnel voyages; leaving the home shores of the UK, sailing through both the Suez and Panama canals, the legendary gilly gilly man, Hong Kong, Singapore, Kobe, Tokyo, and other 'exotic' ports.

We also see and hear the thoughts and memories of some of those who actually sailed with 'Blueys' over their working lives, from Able Seaman to Captain, Steward to Engineer.

'...The film is a must for anyone who sailed with 'Blueys' or who sailed in the merchant navy of old...'   Sea Breezes

Running time approx: 56.00 mins -. £17.95

Blue Funnel - *Voyages and Voices* -Take Two

Blue Funnel
Voyages & Voices
- *Take 2*

After the success of the first Blue Funnel DVD, here is the next one... *Voyages and Voices - Take 2.*

Since the first film ex - Alfred Holt men have popped up all over the world with their amazing old cine footage and photographs. These coupled with more memories of those who actually sailed with Blue Funnel, provide us with another glimpse of what the heydays of the British merchant navy, and in particular Holt's, was like. This time we also include some moving film of the other arm of Holts, the Glen Line or Red Funnel ships, just as important, remembered and revered as their 'blue sisters'.

'...an outstanding DVD....' - Shipping Today & Yesterday

Running time approx: 60.00 mins -. £17.95